Clink
Clank

Kelly Doudna

Consulting Editor, Monica Marx, M.A./Reading Specialist

ABDO
Publishing Company

Published by SandCastle™, an imprint of ABDO Publishing Company, 4940 Viking Drive, Edina, Minnesota 55435.

Printed in the United States.

Credits
Edited by: Pam Price
Curriculum Coordinator: Nancy Tuminelly
Cover and Interior Design and Production: Mighty Media
Photo Credits: Comstock, Corbis Images, Creatas, Digital Vision, Hemera, MetaPhotos, PhotoDisc

Library of Congress Cataloging-in-Publication Data

Doudna, Kelly, 1963-
    Clink clank / Kelly Doudna.
      p. cm. -- (Sound words)
    Includes index.
    Summary: Uses photographs and simple sentences to introduce words that sound like what they mean: whack, splat, splash, clink, slam, thud, bang, clang, whack, crack, smash, crash.
    ISBN 1-59197-451-8
    1. English language--Onomatopoeic words--Juvenile literature. 2. Sounds, Words for--Juvenile literature. [1. English language--Onomatopoeic words. 2. Sounds, Words for.]
I. Title.

PE1597.D635 2003
428.1--dc21

2003044337

SandCastle™ books are created by a professional team of educators, reading specialists, and content developers around five essential components that include phonemic awareness, phonics, vocabulary, text comprehension, and fluency. All books are written, reviewed, and leveled for guided reading, early intervention reading, and Accelerated Reader® programs and designed for use in shared, guided, and independent reading and writing activities to support a balanced approach to literacy instruction.

Let Us Know

After reading the book, SandCastle would like you to tell us your stories about reading. What is your favorite page? Was there something hard that you needed help with? Share the ups and downs of learning to read. We want to hear from you! To get posted on the ABDO Publishing Company Web site, send us e-mail at:

sandcastle@abdopub.com

SandCastle Level: Transitional

Onomatopoeia
(on-uh-mat-uh-**pee**-uh)
is the use of words that
sound like what they
describe.

These **sound words** are
all around us.

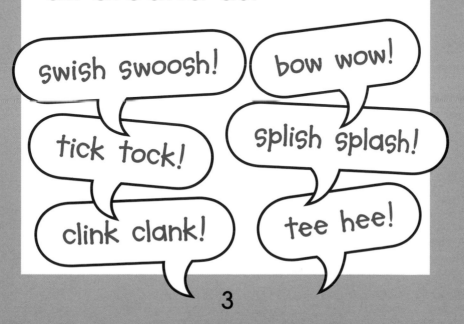

Hal hits a piñata.

Whack!

Steph slaps the wet sponge on the window.

Splat!

Jen jumps into the pool.

Splash!

Tom and Trish tap their glasses together.

Clink!

Shawn shuts the door.

Slam!

Dawn and Donna
drop the books.

Thud!

Crash Bang

bang!

The balloon pops with a bang.

16

The bell rings with a clang.

17

The flyswatter slaps with a whack.

18

The bat smacks the ball with a
crack.

The baseball blasts through the
window with a smash.

The trash can
clatters with a crash.

Picture Index

bang, p. 16

clang, p. 17

slam, p. 13

smash, p. 20

splash, p. 9

whack, pp. 5, 18

Glossary

flyswatter   a piece of mesh attached to a handle that is used to kill flies and other insects

piñata   a decorated container that is filled with candies and gifts and hung from the ceiling, then broken by blindfolded children with sticks

pool   a tank of water that is used for swimming

sponge   a pad that absorbs water and is used for cleaning

About SandCastle™

A professional team of educators, reading specialists, and content developers created the SandCastle™ series to support young readers as they develop reading skills and strategies and increase their general knowledge. The SandCastle™ series has four levels that correspond to early literacy development in young children. The levels are provided to help teachers and parents select the appropriate books for young readers.

Emerging Readers
(no flags)

Beginning Readers
(1 flag)

Transitional Readers
(2 flags)

Fluent Readers
(3 flags)

These levels are meant only as a guide. All levels are subject to change.

ABDO
Publishing Company

To see a complete list of SandCastle™ books and other nonfiction titles from ABDO Publishing Company, visit **www.abdopub.com** or contact us at:

4940 Viking Drive, Edina, Minnesota 55435 • 1-800-800-1312 • fax: 1-952-831-1632